UNDERSTANDING PHILEMON

A COMMENTARY ON THE BOOK OF PHILEMON USING ANCIENT BIBLE STUDY METHODS

Michael Harvey Koplitz

CONTENTS

ACKNOWLEDGMENTS

This work could not have been accomplished without Dr. Anne Davis, who taught me Ancient Bible (Hebraic) study methods, and my two student partners, Rev. Dr. Robert Cook and Pastor Sandra Koplitz. We know that the journey has just started and will last a life time. The discovery of the depths of God's Word is waiting for us to find.

The main differences between the Greek method and Hebraic method of teaching

Once you are aware of the two teaching styles, you will be able to determine if you are in a class or reading a book, whether the analysis and/or teaching method is either in a Greek or Hebraic method. In the Greek method, it is automatically thought that the instructor is right because of advanced knowledge. In the college situation, it is because the professor has his/her Ph.D. in some area of study, so one assumes that he or she knows everything about the topic. For example, Rodney Dangerfield played the role of a middle-aged man going to college. His English midterm was to write about Kurt Vonnegut Jr. Since he didn't understand any of Vonnegut's books he hired Vonnegut himself to the write the midterm. When it was returned to him, the English Professor told Dangerfield that whoever wrote the paper knew nothing about Vonnegut. This is an example of the Greek method of teaching. Did the Ph.D. English professor actually think that she knew more about Vonnegut's writings than Vonnegut did? [1]

In the Greek teaching method, the professor or the instructor claims to be the authority. If you are attending a Bible study class and the class leader says "I will teach you the only way to understand this biblical book," you may want to consider the implications. This method is common since most Seminaries and Bible colleges teach a Greek method of learning, which is the same method the

---

[1] *Back to School*. Performed by Rodney Dangerfield. Hollywood: CA: Paper Clip Productions, 1986. DVD.

church has been utilizing for centuries.

Hebraic teaching methods are different. The teacher wants the students to challenge what they hear. It is through questioning that a student can learn. In addition, the teacher wants his/her students to excel to a point where the student becomes the teacher.

It is said that if two rabbis come together to discuss a passage of Scripture, the result will be at least ten different opinions. All points of view are acceptable as long as the points can be supported by biblical evidence. It is permissible and encouraged for students to have multiple opinions. There is a depth to God's Word, and God wants us to find all of His messages that are placed in the Scriptures.

Seeking out the meaning of the Scriptures beyond the literal meaning is essential to fully understanding God's Word.[2] The Greek method of learning the Scriptures has prevailed over the centuries. One problem is that only the literal interpretation of Scripture was often viewed as valid, as prompted by Martin Luther's "sola literalis" meaning that only the literal interpretation of Scripture was valid. The Fundamentalist movements of today are generally based on the literal interpretation of the Scripture. Therefore, they do not believe that God placed any deeper, hidden, or secret meanings in the Word.

The students of the Scriptures who learn through Hebraic training and understanding

---

[2] Davis, Anne Kimball. *The Synoptic Gospels*. MP3. Albuquerque: NM: BibleInteract, 2012.

have drawn a different conclusion. The Hebrew language itself leads to different possible interpretations because of the construction of the language. The Hebraic method of Bible study opens up avenues of thought about God's revelations in the Scripture that may have never been considered. A question may be raised about the Scripture being studied for which there may not be an immediate answer. If so, it becomes the responsibility of the learners to uncover the meaning. Also, remember that multiple opinions about the meaning of Scripture are also acceptable if they can be supported by Scripture.

METHODOLOGY

The methodology employed is to use First Century Scripture study methods integrated with the customs and culture of Yeshua's day to examine the Hebrew and Christian Scriptures, thus gathering a deeper understanding by learning the Scriptures in the way the people of Yeshua's day did.

The Process of Discovery

I have titled the methodology of analyzing a passage of Scripture in a Hebraic manner the "Process of Discovery." This methodology was developed by the author bringing together the various areas of linguistic and cultural understanding. There are several sections to the process and not all the sections apply to every passage of Scripture. The overall result of developing this process is to give the reader a framework into the ideas being presented.

The "Process of Discovery" starts with a Scripture passage. If the passage is in a poetic form, it is identified. Possible poetic techniques include: parallelism, chiastic structures, and repetition. Formatting the passage in its poetic form allows the reader to be able to visualize what the first century CE listener was hearing. Any parallelism is indicated with colored text and the chiasms are labeled by their corresponding sections, for example: A, B, C, B', A'. Not all passages of the Scriptures have a poetic form.

The next step is to "question the narrative," which is accomplished by assuming the reader knows nothing about the passage. Therefore, the questions go from the simple to the complex. The next task is to identify any linguistic patterns. Linguistic patterns include, but are not limited to: irony, simile, metaphor, symbolism, idioms, hyperbole, figurative language, personification, and allegory.

Any translation inconsistencies discovered between the English NASB version and either the Hebrew or Greek versions are identified. There are times when a Hebrew or Greek word can be translated in more than one way. Inconsistencies also can be created by the translation committee, which may have decided to use traditional language instead of the actual translation. The decision of the translation committee can be generally found in the Preface or Introduction to the Bible. Perhaps some of the inconsistencies were intentionally added to convey some deeper meaning therefore, the inconsistencies need to be examined.

Echoes of the Hebrew Scriptures in the Christian Scripture are identified. This occurs when a passage from the Hebrew Scripture is used in the Christian Scripture or when a command is directly discussed in the Christian Scriptures. [3] In addition, echoes can be found when Torah (Genesis through Deuteronomy) passages are used in other Hebrew Bible books. In addition to echoes, cross references are listed. A cross reference is a reference to another verse in the Scripture which can assist the reader to understand the verse that is being read.

---

[3] Mitzvot are the 613 commandments found in the Torah that please God. There are positive and negative commandments. The list was first development by Maimonides. The full list can be found at: ttp://www.jewfaq.org/613.htm.

The names of persons mentioned in the passage are listed. Many of the Hebrew names have meaning and may be associated with places or actions. Jewish parents used to name their children based on what they felt God had in store for their child. An example of this is Abraham whose original name was Abram, and was changed to mean eternal father (in this case Abram's name was changed by God to Abraham indicating a function he was to perform). When the Hebrew Bible gives names, many of the occurrences will indicate something special to the reader/listener. The same importance can hold true for the names of places. The time it takes to travel between places can supply insight to the event.

Key words are identified in a verse when they are important to an understanding of that passage. There are no rules for selecting the key words. Searching for other occurrences of the keywords in Scripture in a concordance is necessary to understand how the word was being used; this must be done in either Hebrew or Greek, not in English. A classic Hebraic approach is to find the usage of a word in the Scripture by finding other verses that contain the word. The usage of a word, in its original language, is discovered by searching the Scripture in the language of the word. The verses that contain the word being researched are identified and a pattern for the usage of the word is discerned. Each verse is examined to see what the usage of the word is which, may reveal a pattern for the word's usage. For Hebrew words the first usage of the word in the Scripture, especially if used in the Torah, is important. For the Greek words the Christian Scriptures are used to determine the word usage in the Scripture. Sometimes finding the equivalent Greek word in the Septuagint then analyzing its usage in Hebrew can be very helpful.

The Rules of Hillel for Bible understanding can be used when applicable. Hillel was a Torah scholar who lived shortly before Yeshua's day. Hillel developed several rules for Torah students to interpret the Scriptures which are referred to as halachic midrash. In several cases these rules are helpful in the analysis of the Scripture.

After the linguistic analysis is complete an examination of the cultural implications will be examined. The culture is important because it is not specifically referenced in the biblical narratives as indicated earlier.

From the linguistic analysis and the cultural

understanding, it is possible to obtain a deeper meaning of the Scripture beyond the literal meaning of the plain text. That is what the listeners of Yeshua's time were doing. They put the linguistics and the culture together without even having to contemplate it. They simply did it.

This will lead to a conclusion or a set of conclusions about what the passage is talking about. Most of the time the Hebraic analysis leads to the desire for a deeper analysis to fully understand what Yeshua was talking about or what was happening to Him. Whatever the result, a new deeper understanding of the Scripture will be obtained.

The components of the Process of Discovery

are:

Linguistics Section

Linguistic Structure of the Scripture

Discussion

Questioning the Passage

Main/Center Point

Verse Comparison on citations or proof text

Idioms

Metaphors

Symbols

Translation inconsistencies

People's names

Name of places

Word Study

Topics

Scripture cross references

Echoes

Rules of Hillel

Culture Section

Discussion

Questioning the passage culturally

Culture and Linguistics Section

Discussion

Only the sections that are applicable to the Scripture is presented.

The Scripture

New American Standard 1995	Koine Greek	Peshitta
[1] Paul, a prisoner of Christ Jesus, and Timothy our brother, To Philemon our beloved *brother* and fellow worker, [2] and to Apphia our sister, and to Archippus our fellow soldier, and to the church in your	[1] Παῦλος δέσμιος χριστοῦ Ἰησοῦ, καὶ Τιμόθεος ὁ ἀδελφός, Φιλήμονι τῷ ἀγαπητῷ καὶ συνεργῷ ἡμῶν, [2] καὶ Ἀπφίᾳ τῇ ἀγαπητῇ, καὶ Ἀρχίππῳ τῷ συστρατιώτῃ ἡμῶν, καὶ τῇ κατ' οἶκόν σου ἐκκλησίᾳ· [3] χάρις ὑμῖν καὶ εἰρήνη ἀπὸ	[1] PAUL, a prisoner of Jesus the Messiah, and Timothy a brother;--- to the beloved Philemon, a laborer with us, [2] and to our beloved Apphia, and to Archippus a laborer with us, and to

house:

³ Grace to you and peace from God our Father and the Lord Jesus Christ.

⁴ I thank my God always, making mention of you in my prayers,

⁵ because I hear of your love and of the faith which you have toward the Lord Jesus and toward all the saints;

⁶ *and I pray*

θεοῦ πατρὸς ἡμῶν καὶ κυρίου Ἰησοῦ χριστοῦ.

⁴ Εὐχαριστῶ τῷ θεῷ μου, πάντοτε μνείαν σου ποιούμενος ἐπὶ τῶν προσευχῶν μου,

⁵ ἀκούων σου τὴν ἀγάπην, καὶ τὴν πίστιν ἣν ἔχεις πρὸς τὸν κύριον Ἰησοῦν καὶ εἰς πάντας τοὺς ἁγίους,

⁶ ὅπως ἡ κοινωνία τῆς

the church in thy house.

³ Grace be with you, and peace from God our father, and from our Lord Jesus the Messiah.

⁴ I thank my God always, and remember thee in my prayers,

⁵ lo, from the time that I heard of thy faith, and of the love thou

that the fellowship of your faith may become effective through the knowledge of every good thing which is in you for Christ's sake. 7 For I have come to have much joy and comfort in your love, because the hearts of the saints have been refreshed through you, brother. 8 Therefore, though I have	πίστεώς σου ἐνεργὴς γένηται ἐν ἐπιγνώσει παντὸς ἀγαθοῦ τοῦ ἐν ἡμῖν εἰς χριστὸν Ἰησοῦν. 7 Χάριν γὰρ ἔχομεν πολλὴν καὶ παράκλησιν ἐπὶ τῇ ἀγάπῃ σου, ὅτι τὰ σπλάγχνα τῶν ἁγίων ἀναπέπαυται διὰ σοῦ, ἀδελφέ. 8 Διὸ πολλὴν ἐν χριστῷ παρρησίαν ἔχων	hast towards our Lord Jesus, and towards all the saints; 6 that there may be a fellowship of thy faith, yielding fruits in works, and in the knowledge of all the good things ye possess in Jesus the Messiah. 7 For we have great joy and consolation,

enough confidence in Christ to order you *to do* what is proper, 9 yet for love's sake I rather appeal *to you*-- since I am such a person as Paul, the aged, and now also a prisoner of Christ Jesus-- 10 I appeal to you for my child Onesimus, whom I have begotten in my imprisonment,	ἐπιτάσσειν σοι τὸ ἀνῆκον, 9 διὰ τὴν ἀγάπην μᾶλλον παρακαλῶ, τοιοῦτος ὢν ὡς Παῦλος πρεσβύτης, νυνὶ δὲ καὶ δέσμιος Ἰησοῦ χριστοῦ. 10 Παρακαλῶ σε περὶ τοῦ ἐμοῦ τέκνου, ὃν ἐγέννησα ἐν τοῖς δεσμοῖς μου, Ὀνήσιμον, 11 τόν ποτέ σοι ἄχρηστον, νυνὶ δὲ σοὶ καὶ ἐμοὶ	because the bowels of the saints are refreshed by thy love. 8 Therefore I might have great freedom in the Messiah, to enjoin upon thee the things that are right. 9 But for love's sake, I earnestly beseech thee---even I, Paul, who am aged, as thou

[11] who formerly was useless to you, but now is useful both to you and to me. [12] I have sent him back to you in person, that is, *sending* my very heart, [13] whom I wished to keep with me, so that on your behalf he might minister to me in my imprisonment for the gospel; [14] but without your consent I did not want	εὔχρηστον, ὃν ἀνέπεμψα· [12] σὺ δὲ αὐτόν, τοῦτ᾽ ἔστιν τὰ ἐμὰ σπλάγχνα, προσλαβοῦ· [13] ὃν ἐγὼ ἐβουλόμην πρὸς ἐμαυτὸν κατέχειν, ἵνα ὑπὲρ σοῦ διακονῇ μοι ἐν τοῖς δεσμοῖς τοῦ εὐαγγελίου· [14] χωρὶς δὲ τῆς σῆς γνώμης οὐδὲν ἠθέλησα ποιῆσαι, ἵνα μὴ ὡς κατὰ	knowest, and now also a prisoner for Jesus the Messiah. [10] I beseech thee for my son, whom I had begotten in my bonds--- for Onesimus; [11] from whom formerly thou hadst no profit, but now very profitable will he be both to thee

to do anything, so that your goodness would not be, in effect, by compulsion but of your own free will. 15 For perhaps he was for this reason separated *from you* for a while, that you would have him back forever, 16 no longer as a slave, but more than a slave, a beloved	ἀνάγκην τὸ ἀγαθόν σου ᾖ, ἀλλὰ κατὰ ἑκούσιον. 15 Τάχα γὰρ διὰ τοῦτο ἐχωρίσθη πρὸς ὥραν, ἵνα αἰώνιον αὐτὸν ἀπέχῃς· 16 οὐκέτι ὡς δοῦλον, ἀλλ' ὑπὲρ δοῦλον, ἀδελφὸν ἀγαπητόν, μάλιστα ἐμοί, πόσῳ δὲ μᾶλλον σοὶ καὶ ἐν σαρκὶ καὶ ἐν κυρίῳ. 17 Εἰ οὖν με ἔχεις κοινωνόν,	and to me; and whom I have sent to thee. 12 And receive thou him, as one begotten by me. 13 For I was desirous to retain him with me, that he might minister to me in thy stead, in these bonds for the gospel. 14 But I would do nothing

brother, especially to me, but how much more to you, both in the flesh and in the Lord. 17 If then you regard me a partner, accept him as *you would* me. 18 But if he has wronged you in any way or owes you anything, charge that to my account; 19 I, Paul, am writing this with my own hand, I will repay it (not	προσλαβοῦ αὐτὸν ὡς ἐμέ. 18 Εἰ δέ τι ἠδίκησέν σε ἢ ὀφείλει, τοῦτο ἐμοὶ ἐλλόγει· 19 ἐγὼ Παῦλος ἔγραψα τῇ ἐμῇ χειρί, ἐγὼ ἀποτίσω· ἵνα μὴ λέγω σοι ὅτι καὶ σεαυτόν μοι προσοφείλεις. 20 Ναί, ἀδελφέ, ἐγώ σου ὀναίμην ἐν κυρίῳ· ἀνάπαυσόν μου τὰ σπλάγχνα ἐν	without consulting thee; lest thy benefit should be as if by compulsion, and not with thy pleasure. 15 And, perhaps, also, he therefore departed from thee for a season, that thou mightest retain him for ever; 16 henceforth, not as a

to mention to you that you owe to me even your own self as well).

20 Yes, brother, let me benefit from you in the Lord; refresh my heart in Christ.

21 Having confidence in your obedience, I write to you, since I know that you will do even more than what I say.

22 At the same time also

κυρίῳ.

21 Πεποιθὼς τῇ ὑπακοῇ σου ἔγραψά σοι, εἰδὼς ὅτι καὶ ὑπὲρ ὃ λέγω ποιήσεις.

22 Ἅμα δὲ καὶ ἑτοίμαζέ μοι ξενίαν· ἐλπίζω γὰρ ὅτι διὰ τῶν προσευχῶν ὑμῶν χαρισθήσομαι ὑμῖν.

23 Ἀσπάζονταί σε Ἐπαφρᾶς ὁ συναιχμάλωτός μου ἐν χριστῷ Ἰησοῦ,

24 Μάρκος,

servant, but more than a servant, a brother dear to me, and much more to thee, both in the flesh and in our Lord?

17 If therefore thou art in fellowship with me, receive him as one of mine.

18 And if he hath wronged thee, or oweth thee aught, place

prepare me a lodging, for I hope that through your prayers I will be given to you.

23 Epaphras, my fellow prisoner in Christ Jesus, greets you,

24 *as do* Mark, Aristarchus, Demas, Luke, my fellow workers.

25 The grace of the Lord Jesus Christ be with your spirit.

Ἀρίσταρχος, Δημᾶς, Λουκᾶς, οἱ συνεργοί μου.

25 Ἡ χάρις τοῦ κυρίου ἡμῶν Ἰησοῦ χριστοῦ μετὰ τοῦ πνεύματος ὑμῶν. Ἀμήν.

it to my account.

19 I, Paul, have written [it] with my own hand, I will repay:--- not to say to thee, that to me thou owest thy ownself.

20 Yes, my brother, let me be refreshed by thee in our Lord: refresh thou my bowels in the Messiah.

21 Being confident

		that thou wilt hearken to me, I have written to thee: and I know that thou wilt do more than I say.
		22 And herewith, prepare also a house for me to lodge in; for I hope that, by your prayers, I shall be given to you.
		23 Epaphras, a fellow-

		captive with me in Jesus the Messiah, saluteth thee; [24] and Mark, and Aristarchus, and Demas, and Luke, my coadjutors. [25] The grace of our Lord Jesus the Messiah be with your spirit, my brethren.---Amen.

Process of Discovery

Linguistics Section

Linguistic Structure

A [1] Paul, **a prisoner of Christ Jesus**, and Timothy our brother, To Philemon our beloved *brother* and fellow worker, [2] and to Apphia our sister, and to Archippus our fellow soldier, and to the church in your house: [3] Grace to you and peace from God our Father and the Lord Jesus Christ.

B [4] I thank my God always, making mention of you in my prayers, [5] because I hear of your love and of the faith which you have toward the Lord Jesus and toward all the saints; [6] *and I pray* that the fellowship of your faith may become effective through the knowledge of every good thing which is in you for Christ's sake. [7] For I have come to have much joy and comfort in your love, because **the hearts of the saints have been refreshed** through you, brother.

C [8] Therefore, though I have enough

confidence in Christ to order you *to do* what is proper, [9] yet for love's sake I rather appeal *to you*-- since **I am such a person as Paul**, the aged, and now also a prisoner of Christ Jesus—

D [10] I appeal to you for my child Onesimus, whom I have begotten in my imprisonment, [11] who formerly was useless to you, but now is useful both to you and to me. [12] **I have sent him back to you in person**, that is, *sending* my very heart, [13] whom I wished to keep with me, so that on your behalf he might minister to me in my imprisonment for the gospel; [14] but without your consent I did not want to do anything, so that your goodness would not be, in effect, by compulsion but of your own free will.

E [15] For perhaps he was for this reason separated *from you* for a while, that you would have him back forever, [16] no longer as a slave, but more than a slave, a beloved brother, especially to me, but how much more to you, both in the flesh and in the Lord.

D' [17] If then you regard me a partner, **accept him as *you would* me.** [18] But if he has wronged you in any way or owes you anything, charge that to my account;

C' [19] **I, Paul, am writing this with my own hand**, I will repay it (not to mention to you that you owe to me even your own self as well).

B' [20] Yes, brother, let me benefit from you in the Lord; **refresh my heart in Christ**. [21] Having confidence in your obedience, I write to you, since I know that you will do even more than what I say. [22] At the same time also prepare me a lodging, for I hope that through your prayers I will be given to you.

A' [23] Epaphras, **my fellow prisoner in Christ Jesus**, greets you, [24] *as do* Mark, Aristarchus, Demas, Luke, my fellow workers. [25] The grace of the Lord Jesus Christ be with your spirit.

Discussion

This is a very short letter which Paul wrote to Onesimus on behalf of Philemon. The letter is one very larger chiasm. Since the letter does not describe the entire situation we can only infer how it started.

Questioning the narrative

(Answers to these questions are offered for discussion purposes and you may have different answers. Remember, answers must be defendable from Scripture. In addition, you may have additional questions about the passage that is not covered. This applies to this section and to the Questioning the

Passage in the Cultural section.)

1. Who is Philemon, Apphia, and Achippus, and how does Paul know him? (v. 1)

   It is not known how Paul knew these people. Since Paul does refer to them as fellow workers he must have met them when he established a church in their town. From their names these three people are probably Greeks. This statement must be tempered because Hellenist Jews did name their children with Greek names. They have a house church as indicated in verse two.

2. Why is Archippus called a fellow soldier? (v. 2)

Refer to the Word Study section - συστρατιώτης. Since Paul used this term for Archippus there must have been a difference between the work that he did versus the work that the sisters did. Perhaps it was the task of the sisters to keep the house church running, while it might have been Achippus' task to evangelize. Since the word συστρατιώτης is used only twice in the Christian Scriptures we will never know the exact reason Paul wrote this they. There is also the possibility that Archippus did not feel that he was accomplishing anything for Yeshua and Paul's words may have brought some comfort.

3. What are the good things which is in you for Christ's sake in verse 6?

Good things are those actions and preaching that is done for the spreading of the Gospel of Yeshua.

4. Who are the saints? (v. 7)

Saints are persons who reach as close to perfection in Yeshua, as is humanly possible. During Paul's time, the saints were leading the churches that he had established. With the growth of the church, the leaders of the churches must have been blessed as saints to keep it all going.

5. What does it mean to be a prisoner in Christ? (v. 9)

Refer to the Word Study section - δέσμιος – before reading further. To be a prisoner in Christ could mean that one has committed an offense against Yeshua. In the same manner if one committed a crime against the Kingdom, that individual would become a prisoner of the King. An example is the Genesis story of Joseph who became a prisoner of the Pharaoh. Being a prisoner of the King, Joseph was bound to the will of the King. Therefore, being a prisoner in Christ means that through a crime, the committing a sin, Paul became bound to Yeshua because the sin was against God and Yeshua. Being now bound to Yeshua meant that he was obligated to do the will of Yeshua. Paul searched out the early Jewish followers of Yeshua and brought them before the Sanhedrin for judgment. That was Paul's main crime against Yeshua. On the road to Damascus Paul became Yeshua's prisoner because of that sin. Then bound by Yeshua he did Yeshua's work as Yeshua commanded him. God's grace is shown clearly since none of us who are prisoners in Yeshua are placed into a real prison. Instead we receive forgiveness and salvation. It must be remembered that the forgiven sinner is still a prisoner, that is bound, to Yeshua.

6. Who was Onesimus? (v. 10)

"ONESIMUS [ō nĕs´ məs] (Gk.*Onēsimos* "useful"). A slave, presumably of Philemon, who apparently stole from his master and fled to Rome, where he met Paul (Phlm. 10). There Onesimus became a Christian and a "son" to the imprisoned apostle, who later returned him to Philemon with a letter (the epistle to Philemon). In the letter Paul commends Onesimus, offers to personally compensate Philemon for his loss, and conveys his hope that Onesimus can continue to serve him (vv. 10–20). Playing on the name Onesimus, Paul writes that the slave formerly "useless" to

Philemon had become "useful" to both (v. 11). Onesimus is mentioned also at Col. 4:9 as "one of yourselves" among those whom Paul sent to bear the epistle.

Employing the same pun as Paul, Ignatius of Antioch commends in a letter to Ephesus *ca.* A.D. 115 a bishop named Onesimus. The name, however, appears to have been common, first among slaves and then among Christians commemorating Paul's associate. It is not impossible that the person named by Ignatius was the biblical figure, but were he still alive he would have been a very old man.

Some scholars suggest that Onesimus is to be identified with ONESIPHORUS, of which his name could be a shortened form (cf. *Onēsiphoros* "profit-bearing"). Like Onesimus, Onesiphorus ministered to the imprisoned Paul at Rome (2 Tim. 1:16–17). He also apparently was active at Ephesus (v. 18)."[4]

7. What does "sending my very heart" mean? (v. 12)

Paul decided to send Onesimus back to Philemon (refer to the Culture section). Paul could not go with him because he was in a Roman prison. Therefore, he sent

---

[4] Myers, A. C. (1987). In *The Eerdmans Bible dictionary* (p. 781). Grand Rapids, MI: Eerdmans.

his heart meaning, Paul was with Onesimus in spirit.

8. Why was Philemon separated from Onesimus and what problem did it cause? (v. 15)

It is not known why Onesimus ran away from Philemon. Probably Onesimus was not happy about his treatment since both Onesimus and Philemon become followers of Yeshua. Possibly Onesimus expected to be released from his imprisonment to Philemon.

9. Why is Philemon asked to accept Onesimus as Philemon would welcome Paul? (v. 17)

Philemon is asked not to punish

Onesimus for leaving without permission.

10. Why does Paul tell Onesimus that he wrote the letter with his own hand? (v. 19)

In Paul's day, a disciple of Paul could write a letter and sign the name "Paul." In this letter Paul has made it clear that he, Paul, penned the letter.

11. Why are some of the people mentioned have different titles? (general question)

They might have had different positions, or responsibilities in the church. This could have been the start of clergy versus lay persons, etc.

Main/Center Point

From the E clause of the chiasm there is a call for Philemon to consider Onesimus as an equal. Inside of the faith of Yeshua everyone is equal. There is not supposed to be any ranks. Each of us fits into the body of Yeshua performing different tasks. Society has its ranks and hierarchies but the church of Yeshua should not.

Idioms

1. "put it on (charge it to) my account" (v. 18)

This Near Eastern idiom means to "forget it." "In the Near East, when a man makes an appeal on behalf of a friend or a poor person, he speaks very frankly and uses peculiar expressions." [5]

People's names

1. **Παῦλος** *Paulos* **Meaning:** (Sergius) *Paulus* (a Roman proconsul), also *Paul* (an apostle)

2. **Ἰησοῦς** *Iesous* **Meaning:** *Jesus* or *Joshua*, the name of the Messiah

3. **Τιμόθεος** *Timotheos* **Meaning:** Timothy, a Christian

4. **Φιλήμων** *Philemon* **Meaning:** 'kindly,' *Philemon*, a Christian

5. **Ἀπφία** *Apphia* **Meaning:** *Apphia*, a Christian woman in Colossae

---

[5] Errico, Rocco A., and George M. Lamsa. "Philemon." *Aramaic Light on Galatians through Hebrews: A Commentary Based on Aramaic, the Language of Jesus, and Ancient Near Eastern Customs.* Smyma, GA: Noohra Foundation, 2005. N. pag. Print.

6. Ἄρχιππος *Archippos* **Meaning:** 'horse-ruler,' *Archippus,* a Christian at Colossae

7. Ὀνήσιμος *Onesimos* **Meaning:** 'useful,' *Onesimus,* a Christian

8. Ἐπαφρᾶς *Epaphras* **Meaning:** Epaphras, a Christian

9. **Μάρκος** *Markos* **Meaning:** *Mark,* a Christian

10. Ἀρίσταρχος *Aristarchos* **Meaning:** 'best leader,' *Aristarchus,* a Christian of Thessalonica

11. **Δημᾶς** *Demas* **Meaning:** Demas, a companion of Paul

12. **Λουκᾶς** *Loukas* **Meaning:** Luke, a Christian

Word Study

1. **δέσμιος** *desmios* **Meaning:** binding, bound (v. 9)

   > [NAU] **Matthew 27:15** Now at *the* feast the governor was accustomed to release for the people *any* one **prisoner** whom they wanted. (Matt. 27:15 NAU)

   > [NAU] **Mark 15:6** Now at *the* feast he used to release for them *any* one **prisoner** whom they requested. (Mk. 15:6 NAU)

   > [NAU] **Acts 16:25** But about midnight Paul and Silas were praying and singing hymns of **praise** to God, and the prisoners were listening to them; (Acts 16:25 NAU)

   Conclusion: *demios* is consistently used in the Christian Scriptures as "prisoner." However, it can also mean to bind oneself to another person. Since being a prisoner has a negative connotation it might be valuable to look at the Hebraic concept of being bound to a person.

אָסִיר *asir*   **Meaning:** *a bondman, prisoner*

[NAU] **Genesis 39:20** So Joseph's master took him and put him into the jail, the place where the king's prisoners were confined; and he was there in the jail. (Gen. 39:20 NAU)

[NAU] **Judges 16:21** Then the Philistines seized him and gouged out his eyes; and they brought him down to Gaza and bound him with bronze chains, and he was a grinder in the prison. (Jdg. 16:21 NAU)

[NAU] **Job 3:18** "The prisoners are at ease together; They do not hear the voice of the taskmaster. (Job 3:18 NAU)

Conclusion: The   English

translations use the word "prisoner" in just about every case. A synonym is "to be bound" is offered in the Theological Wordbook of the Old Testament.[6]

2. συστρατιώτης *sustratiotes* **Meaning:** a fellow soldier (v. 2)

[NAU] **Philippians 2:25** But I thought it necessary to send to you Epaphroditus, my brother and fellow worker and fellow soldier, who is also your messenger and minister to my need; (Phil. 2:25 NAU)

This word is only found in Philippians and Philemon. That does not give enough information

---

[6] Harris, R. Laird, Gleason L. Archer, and Bruce K. Waltke. "Asir." In *Theological Wordbook of the Old Testament*. Chicago, IL.: Moody Press, 1980.

to develop a pattern for the usage of the word.

From BDAG: συστρατιώτης, ου, ὁ (s. στρατιώτης; X., Pla. et al.; BGU 814, 27 [soldier's letter]; O. Wilck II, 1535 [II BC]; Jos., Ant. 4, 177) *comrade in arms, fellow-soldier,* in our lit. only fig. of those who devote themselves to the service of the gospel; as a term of honor (which in Polyaenus 8, 23, 22 makes the soldier equal to the commander-in-chief, and in Synes., Kingship 13 p. 12c makes the warrior equal to the king) applied to certain of Paul's associates mentioned in **Phil 2:25; Phlm 2** (on the Christian life as military service s. πανοπλία 2).— DELG s.v. στρατός. M-M. TW. [7]

---

[7] Danker, Frederick W., Walter Bauer, and William F. Arndt. "Sustratiotes." *A Greek-English Lexicon of the New Testament and Other Early Christian Literature.* Chicago: U of Chicago, 2000. N. pag.

Scripture cross references

Verse 2   Rom 16:1 Col 4:17, Phi 2:25; 2Ti 2:3, Rom 16:5

Verse 4   Rom 1:8f

Verse 5   Eph 1:15; Col 1:4; 1Th 3:6

Verse 6   Phi 1:9; Col 1:9; Col 3:10

Verse 7   2Co 7:4, 2Co 7:13; 1Co 16:18

Verse 9   Gal 3:26; 1Ti 1:12;

Verse 10   Rom 12:1; 1Co 4:14f; Col 4:9

Verse 14   2Co 9:7; 1Pe 5:2

Verse 19   1Co 16:21; 2Co 10:1; Gal 5:2; 2Co 9:4

Verse 22   Act 28:23, Phi 1:25; Phi 2:24; 2Co 1:11; Act 27:24; Heb 13:19

Verse 24   Act 12:12, Act 12:25; Act 15:37-39; Col 4:10; Act 19:29; Act 27:2; Col 4:10;

Col 4:14; 2Ti 4:10f

Verse 25   Gal 6:18; 2Ti 4:22

Culture Section
Discussion

"In the eastern part of the Roman Empire during this period, fugitive slaves who sought sanctuary in a household were likely to be given temporary protection by the householder until either a reconciliation with the master had been effected or else the slave had been put up for sale in the market and the resulting price paid to the owner (Goodenough, *HTR* 22 [1929] 181–83, drew attention to an Athenian law to this effect; it is suggested that this provision survived in Egypt under the Ptolemies and well into Roman imperial times as it influenced Ulpian's legislation early in the third century A.D.). The relevant Deuteronomic law ran as follows: "you shall not give up to his master a slave who has escaped from his master to you; he shall dwell with you, in your midst, in the place which he shall choose within one of your towns, where it pleases him best; you shall not oppress him" (Deut 23:15, 16). Although this law carried divine authority for Paul, as Bruce (*Paul*, 400) notes, "he would not invoke it without Philemon's consent, preferring Philemon to act like a Christian of his own free will" (note Bruce's whole discussion, *Paul*, 399, 400)."[8]

"Chattel slavery, in which the slave-

---

[8] O'Brien, P. T. (1998). *Colossians, Philemon* (Vol. 44, pp. 292–293). Dallas: Word, Incorporated.

owner had absolute or nearly absolute control over the slave, was widespread in the Roman Empire."[9]

Culture and Linguistics Section
Discussion

Paul is asking Philemon to do him a favor and not to punish Onesimus for running away as a fugitive slave. In addition, the point Paul was making is that those who are bound to Yeshua are equal in Yeshua's eye. Paul accepts that there is a hierarchy to society however, there is no hierarchy in Heaven.

Thoughts

We are bound to Yeshua our Messiah because of the sins we have committed against the commandments and ordinances of our God. When we sin, we sin against Yeshua. To receive forgiveness for sins we give ourselves over to Yeshua. We do become prisoners of Yeshua because in our baptism we give up our old selves and become what Yeshua wants us to be. Being bound to Yeshua means following Yeshua's teaching about the Torah and the commandments of God. Being a prisoner of Yeshua is a good thing. Think of it as being bound to Yeshua. One belongs to Yeshua through one's faith and because one becomes a prisoner of the Messiah, one then is being a true follower. Being a prisoner (bound) of Yeshua is how to receive the grace of forgiveness from our God.

Also, there is no hierarchy in the church

nor the kingdom of God when it comes to our souls. Every member of the church has a specific contribution to make and no one is of higher rank than anyone else. We are all equal in Yeshua's eye.

Bibliography

Bauer-Danker, Greek-English Lexicon of the NT (BDAG). (2016, 2 17).

Danker, F. W. (2000). *A Greek-English Lexicon of the New Testament and Other Early Christian Literature.* Chicago: Univerity of Chicago.

Davis, A. K. (2012). The Synoptic Gospels. Albuquerque.

Errico, R. A. (2005). *Aramaic Light on Galatians through Hebrews: A commentary based on Aramaic.* Smyma, GA: Noohra Foundation.

Harris, R. L. (1980). *Theological Wordbook of the Old Testament.* Chicago: IL: Moody Press.

Myers, A. (1987). *The Eerdmans BIble Dictionary.* Grand Rapids, MI: Eerdmans Publishing.

O'Brien, P. (1998). *Colossians, Philemon.* Dallas, TX: Word Incorporated.

Signorelli, J. (Director). (1986). *Back to School* [Motion Picture].